MINE

DIARY OF A ZOMBIE PIGMAN

Alex Brian

☐ Copyright 2015 by Alex Brian

All rights reserved.
No part of this publication may be reproduced
in any way whatsoever, without written permission
from the author, except in case of brief
quotations embodied in critical reviews
and articles.
First edition, 2015

Disclaimer:

This unofficial Minecraft novel is an original work of fan fiction which
is not sanctioned nor approved by the makers of Minecraft.
Minecraft is a registered trademark of, and owned by, Mojang AB,
and its respective owners, which do not authorize, sponsor, or endorse this book.
All names, characters, places, and other aspects of
the game described herein are owned and
trademarked by their respective owners.

Thank You For Downloading This Book!

[Click Here For More Minecraft Diaries By Amazon's Best Selling Author 'Alex Brian'!](http://amzn.to/1GkHjxB)

Or Go To:

http://amzn.to/1GkHjxB

I'm a Zombie Pigman, and it's AWESOME. The Nether is such a great place!

The deafening gurgle and screech of the Ghasts overhead, the grunts of my fellow Zombie Pigmen, and the crackling song of the entire world being on fire... ah, it's all so soothing and wonderful.

I especially like to head down to the beach and lay out by the lava, watching it bubble and roll.

I hear it goes down forever, but no one really knows. I asked around, but no one knew-- not even the little Squeals.

Things are pretty simple, here in the Nether. No one's ever really angry.

The Wither Skeletons get along with the Blazes, the Zombie Pigmen get along with the Magma Cubes, and everyone has a good time.

Sometimes we hang out in the

Fortresses dotted over the landscape of the Nether.

I really like hanging out with the Blazes. It's fun to watch them fly around, I think. They never get quite as high as the Ghasts, but they're not giant puffballs of concentrated flame either!

I'd like to show you my diary. I'm sure it will give you a great idea about what it's really like to live in the Nether.

When you're done, you're sure to want to come and visit us, just like that weird pink fellow did.

Table Of Contents

Day 1

Day 2

Day 3

Day 4

Day 5

Day 6

Day 7

Preview Of Amazon Best Seller 'Diary Of A Minecraft Creeper by Alex Brian'

Day 1:

What a wonderful day to be a Zombie Pigman. The Glowstone is humming, the lava is bubbling, the Ghast is shrieking, and the ground is dotted with sections of roaring flame.

I woke up from my standing nap, grabbed my gold sword, and set out to explore like I always do.

Really, there are only a few different kinds of things to see in the Nether, but there are so many of them that it's really worth seeing them all!

I've been seeing a lot of Nether Quartz lately. Ah, I wish my gold sword wasn't so soft and bendy. It would be really fun to...

I don't know, get it out of there somehow, make something out of it.

Maybe even a better sword! All these

gold nuggets, and no Nether Quartz. No fair.

Day 2:

Found another Nether Fortress today! This one is a lot like the others, except it has this weird purple gate in it. I've never seen one of those before!

I walked around, said hi to all the Blazes and Magma Cubes and Wither Skeletons, all the usual stuff.

The paths went on for so long that I almost didn't find my way back to that entrancing gate.

I could hear something really weird coming from the other side, over the groaning and whooshing of the gate itself.

It sounded like... iron on stone, some chipping, grinding, popping thing.

I can't imagine what could possibly be on the other side, but I'm not entirely sure I want to know, really!

...Or do I? I might go through it tomorrow. Why not, right?

Day 3:

I really shouldn't have gone through that gate.

The moment I stepped out, I was absolutely frozen-- both with fear and with... well, cold.

I couldn't feel any lava nearby.

There were no fires. No Glowstone

shining down its bright warmth from above.

I was alone in some... underground... something.

It was grey, and I was stuck behind a door. Through the slit in the door, I saw him. His shirt was some terrifying color of... anti-red.

I've never seen anything like it, but I think it might be "blue". His skin was kinda colored like mine, but it all seemed to be in one piece. How bizarre.

He saw me, and immediately turned around and ran up the stairs.

It was so dark in there after he made the light go away.

I have no idea what those red wire things are, or the square light-boxes they're attached to.

All I know is, he touched some stick,

and all the lights went out. What kind of powerful evil does he wield?

I couldn't stay in the cold and dark anymore, so I went back through the gate.

Ah, that rush of boiling air, the scent of rolling lava and Blaze fumes... this is home.

Forget that place. I'm going to pretend I never went through.

Day 4:

Maybe I should have stayed on the other side.

I saw that weird pink man again today. This time, he was running around the Fortress, knocking the blocks off of some of the walls and collecting them.

I didn't even know that things could

be damaged that way! It was an absolute revolution. He took the window pieces, the walls, even some of the floors.

Every time he knocked a piece off, he'd pick it up and put it in his pocket.

Just how deep are those things? He tore down almost an entire tower, and every bit of it fit in his pockets!

Maybe I could convince him to use

that pointy thing to get some Nether Quartz for me? I really could use that new sword.

I decided not to bother him today. He's a weird one, though.

After running around for a while, he knocked a wall down and jumped to the ground outside.

Then, he built a high pillar from Netherrack and knocked down a bunch of Glowstone with his two-part pointy thing.

I watched for a long time, then decided to follow him. I stayed far back so he wouldn't think I was being weird. After a while, he finally did it!

He hit Nether Quartz with his pointy thing! Oh, I was so happy.

It only took him moments, and the Netherrack exploded and sent the quartz spinning from it.

He picked every bit up though, so I went to ask him if he would share.

I guess one of my fellow Pigmen had the same idea, but when he got too close, I guess the pink man got scared, turned around, pulled out a sword, and hit him with it!

Oh, and what a sword it was-- made from some incredible blue material, shimmering and shining in the low lava-light.

I'd never seen anything like it, really.

Well, as you might imagine, the other Pigman didn't like that very much, and neither did the hundred other Zombie Pigmen around.

They rushed him with their soft gold swords, but they couldn't really do much but chase him back through that big gate.

It was kinda funny, he spent a long time just perched on top of another column he made, just out of their reach.

I guess I'm just not as violent as the others, but he really did kinda make me mad!

I'm gonna have to give him a piece of my mind when he comes back through here.

Day 5:

I should have been watching more carefully. Oh, man... this isn't good.

He took it all. All of it. He took the Glowstone, every bit of it. He took the Nether Quartz too, every vein chipped and chopped dry.

I walked in each direction for a long time, looking for him or any sign that he'd left any for the rest of us. Nothing. Absolutely nothing.

Well, not nothing-- there were plenty of fires, and sticks on fire, and large towers of strange brown and grey materials.

It was all such an ugly contrast with our beloved red.

He'd made huge holes in the ground digging out all the Quartz, and everyone had to be careful to step around them, otherwise they wouldn't be able to get out.

He carved deep tunnels into our beautiful mountains and hills, for who knows what reason.

Just... so long, extending way past what I could see, full of those weird sticks. No way I was gonna go down there.

It's so hard to believe that anyone

could do this in such a short period of time, but I watched how quickly he worked.

He's really made an eye sore of this area, both with his weird towers popping up everywhere and his constant digging and chipping away at our Netherrack and Quartz and Glowstone.

I can't stop thinking about the way he did it, though. Come to think of it, his two-point thing was made of that same incredible blue material his sword was.

What is this other-worldly stuff? Maybe I've been thinking about the wrong thing this whole time. Maybe I need a sword made of *that*.

I think I'd like his picker thing too. It's kinda like... a picking axe or something. Snort.

I have to figure out how to get it away from him without being too mean about it. I couldn't just run up and take it or anything!

Day 6:

Well, he came again today. I watched him come through the gate, and... well, I wanted to stop him, I really did!

But I couldn't bring myself to hit him or anything until he did something to me.

Wouldn't you know it, he walked

right past me like I wasn't even there! He must have known I was too scared to do it.

I still followed him, though. I watched him run around and steal the heads right off of the harmless Wither Skeletons.

What kind of person does that? What could he possibly want with their heads? I mean, how are they doing to see where they're going now?

I know they didn't have eyes or anything, but I'm pretty sure they used their heads to see. Somehow.

I watched him stand right next to the Blaze spawning area and knock them down, too.

When he hit them with that sword, they just fell down and turned into powder. Can you believe that?

He chased the Magma Cubes down and squished them into weird

Magma Cream.

Oh, I wanted to stop him so bad, but until he hit me or one of my friends, I just... couldn't! I don't know what was was stopping me, but I'll definitely be braver next time.

After all that, he went back through the gate-- I guess to drop off all the stuff he stole-- then came back. You wouldn't believe it!

He even had the audacity to take out

this crazy contraption that shot long skinny bolts of something and attack the Ghast!

He didn't get away with that one, though. BOOM! Big fireball, hehehe. It's about time.

It left a big hole in the ground, and no matter how hard I looked, I couldn't find that guy.

You know what I did find, though? All his stuff! Well, I mean, I couldn't very well just run in and take it all. I did wait for a little while to see if he would come back.

I think maybe he did and the Wither Skeletons got him, because I heard a lot of rustling and bone clanking from the direction of the gate. So funny.

So, now I've got not only a shiny blue picking-axe, but a really great new sword too! Today is the best day.

Day 7:

Well, I guess he's not coming back. Seems like he got everything he wanted from the Nether.

He took the Wither Skeletons' heads, the Blazes' powder, the Magma Cubes' cream, all the Glowstone he could get his hands on, every bit of Nether Quartz in the area around the Fortress, and even some gold nuggets and swords.

He even closed off the gate from the other side so we couldn't come find him and take our stuff back.

I'm alright, though. I've got a bunch of new stuff, and all the time in the world to figure out how to use it.

I'll be the envy of all my Pigmen friends when I figure out what this weird circle thing with the spinning red stick inside is.

Well, that's my diary from the last week. Pretty interesting, right?

You wouldn't believe how much fun we have in the Nether, even when things get kinda weird like they did with that guy.

You should definitely come and visit us sometime.

I'll introduce you to the Magma Cubes. They give the best hugs.

************** The End

****

Preview Of Amazon Best Seller 'Diary Of A Minecraft Creeper by Alex Brian'

Day 1

I think I was born today! The first creepy memory I have is of my heartbeat, a faint ticking sound beneath my chest.

I couldn't feel it, I do not have arms. Hey, wait a second...I don't have ears either... But I could certainly hear it! It was so creepy.

I saw my reflection in a little pond nearby, black holes for eyes and a crooked smile. I truly was a Creeper.

Ahead of me, I saw a vast landscape

of trees and grass. Confused as to what my purpose was, I listened closer to my heartbeat.

Tick, Tick, Tick. I am unsure how I just appeared here or what I should do. This is all just so creepy, I feel like wandering around in circles until I find a real purpose.

This is my diary, the Diary of A Creeper. I have decided that since today is the day I was born, today would be my Birthday.

Happy Creepy Birthday to me! I should write down everything I know, like a memoir. I will walk in circles the rest of the night until I figure out what I should do next.

Click Here To Read More!

Or Go To: http://amzn.to/1BZqO7F

MORE MINECRAFT DIARIES BY AMAZON'S BEST SELLING AUTHOR 'ALEX BRIAN'

Click Here For More Books By Alex Brian!

Or Go To:
http://amzn.to/1GkHjxB